# Note To Self
## It's just an existential crisis

Kelley Farrell

ISBN-13: 9798642231821

Library of Congress Control Number: 2018675309
Printed in the United States of America

# SOMETHING MORE

I'm tempted to let the earth swallow
me whole
To sink into oceans of dirt
Slide through the fissures at the core
And come out on the other side
Something more

# FLOURISH

I'm terrified
This is everything
Life was meant to be

# THE STARS MUST KNOW

Do we ever truly know
What it is to be alone
Until we've entangled
With a soul in which we see our own?
The stars must know,
For they once were one.
Split apart by time,
A slow violent upending.
Now they beam in the night,
A call to the halves once held near.
Don't forget,
We're still floating out here.
Apart we may be,
Bound by constraints unseen
But connected in the fabric of every
being.

## I AM

I am broken bloodied nails on a brick
wall.
I am lines and lines and lines of
cocaine.
I am silent screams never heard over
rumbling trains.
I am lanes of cars flying aimlessly
towards oblivion.
I am thousands of black holes existing
in one.
I am the oceans weaving, waving edge.
I am a body in a shallow grave
Eyes open, tongue split and breath
spent.
I am a girl with a carefully laced
valentine
Waiting, waiting, but I'm afraid this is
it.

# AMNESIA

I remember the days,
Like small grains of sand
In folds of skin.
Fuzzy photographs
Taken in the dark,
Subjects on the move.
I know we were there
But can't quite tell.
Maybe it's in the blur of arms
Or a tangling of legs.
I can feel your memory
A stray hair
Sliding between my fingers.

SUBSCRIPTION

I signed up for more.
It seems they lost the paperwork.
I can reason it away.
What's life but missed words?
I'd cancel early but the fee is too high.

# SIX WORD STORIES FROM THE VOID

Nothing but a whiney little bitch
Nothing but a snot nosed snitch
Should've been a boy, stupid girl
Should've been stronger, weak little shit.
For sale: broken heart; completely shattered.
Just get over it, little witch.

# LORD KNOWS

There's something written in the
heavens, stolen by your pen. Lord
knows it'll be a masterpiece once
returned again.
All great poets ascended to the stars,
Leaving wisdom on a path that is ours.
How shall you find it and what should
you do?
My love, the Gods have plagiarized
you.
Voices like honey and ink that scrolls
divine,
Does nothing to betray the beauty of
words you find.
Like all great loves they must pass
through your inkwell, finding salvation.
But still the question falls, what ever
shall you do?
My love, the stars saw inside and stole
the very words we struck out to
enshrine.

For there was something written in the heavens, stolen by your pen. Lord knows, it'll be a masterpiece once returned again.

# SOAKED TO THE BONE

It starts with a low buzzing
A light humming,
Echoing, bouncing, off the bricked
walls of my mind.
Quickly it grows, a wildfire
Clanging and banging along the barred
windows of my soul.
It cannot be freed.
It will not be unleashed.
But the steady clash grows,
A cacophonous symphony of
chainsaws
Hacking away at the binding of my
heart.
Reaching a crescendo,
There's only one way to stop it now.
Ripping away at the flesh that holds us,
Stabbing forth the hearts that blind us,
The deeds are done, the buzz has gone,
Soaked to the bone,
In the blood of a crescendo.

# WHISPER YOUR NAME

Today,
I almost said your name.
A ghost haunting the doors to my
mind,
You're always there but rarely do I find
...
Today,
I almost didn't whisper to the clouds.
Instead I choked on the word,
Fearful that somehow you'd hear.
Our greatest fear has always been
falling.
Today, I almost hit the ground.

# NUMBERED DAYS

My heart could be filled
But truth be told
My days are numbered here.
This disease is terminal.
"Well," he says
Dropping words like porridge over
spindly hands
"You can't stay forever in the land of
the damned."
Indeed Father Time.
It appears I've been diagnosed with life.
I can't stop my feet from wandering
Or my mind from pandering
The sweet effects of a sunset over the
sea.
Suddenly, it seems,
I have things I need to be
Rather than this old burnt out bag of
flesh
And crumbling calcium deposits
collected for me.

# THREADS OF GOLD

I want to lie between the lines
To feel the words moving and sinking
Gnashing and gnawing
I want to sink into the crevices between
melodies
The breaths between chords
To feel the rhythms beating and
crashing
Tearing and thrashing
I inhale every heartbroken word
Let it sink into my skin
A permanent tattoo
Too strong to break
Too fragile to hold
Something nurtured in the dark
Until it becomes too bold
Let the waves crash over me
Stripping my spirit clean
Sew my pieces with your song

# I GUESS IT'S IMPROVEMENT

My head hurt
So I just kept drinking.
Now I can't feel
My tongue
Or my heart,
Or the ache
I've buried
Deep under this art.
But the tears keep coming
Like I'm mourning.
I guess its improvement
Since before
I didn't feel
Anything at all.

# TIPTOE THE LINE

I tiptoe the line
Between the ever converging
Gold and brown of your eye.
I balance so fine
On the hair pin moments
Of raised voices and tender kisses.
One day I'll swan dive
Into the crushing distinctions,
Bringing reality rushing over
daydreams.
For now
I dance the edge of a dime,
Spinning through scenes
Painted like oil slicks on my mind.

# INK ME DOWN

Sink me into paper
Until ink bleeds
Over your finger.
Go ahead,
Ink me down.  Grind memories into
nothing
With razor blade stones.
Release me with every breath.
Let every sound have a bite.
Scream the words
Over glazed eyes and tear stained faces.
Go ahead,
Ink me down.
Your best tragedy,
Your personal comedy.

# PARDON ME

I'm sorry,
What is it I'm radiating?
I don't look happy?
What was that sigh, you ask?
Pardon me.
Let me zip it, clip it
Put it back together.
I forgot.
Falling apart here
Is dipping in waters well known.
Excuse me.
My fault for displaying
Any emotion but what you feel.
You know I can't read minds
But no,
You just don't care.
Let me zip it, clip it
Put it back together here.

# LOVERS

A moth flutters by the light,
Off into the night.
A lover's hand travels slowly
Tracing gentle, dancing lines
Tickling, teasing
Over her craving body.
His lips pull forth her secrets.
Fingers intertwine.
A space made for one another
Under cover of time.
Birds sit on a line,
A world unaware.

HALLOWED HALLS

I'm afraid of the memory you left
behind,
Of trembling shadows racing down the
hall.
Every breath you ever dared me to
breathe,
Beats against stagnating dust on the
wall
Whipping up storms, clogging my
lungs.
I curl the emotions of a scared little girl
Into a fragile ball
And bounce it until it shatters
Against the foundations
Of a house never really built.
Now what's left?
A childhood picture-less and torn
With the bruises of spilled milk and
stairs never existing when we fall.

# SYNC

One moment is all it takes,
The synchronous flow of our souls
Disturbs the very way air flows.

ALWAYS

I woke up today
With your arms pulling me closer,
Your hands running over my hips,
Sliding lower,
Teasing me as you're apt to do.
I woke up to your laugh,
Your lips on my neck
And shoulders
And lower ...
Until I woke up today.

# WE ARE LADIES (IN ALL BUT MAKE)

I am frozen.
A shadow against your light.
A doubt
Buried under the weight of your greed.
I am all but cast aside,
A pawn to be thrust every which way.
I step lightly
Across your back.
I stomp violently over the cracks.
We are ladies in all but make.
Soothe our skirts.
Remind us again,
With supple bruised skin,
What's at stake.

# 136 UNTITLED DRAFTS

Depression is 136 untitled drafts
Neatly ordered by cut and depth,
Catalogued by tears spread
And self-destroying claims.
It's reflections,
No longer resembling the party,
And freezing floors
Under burning drunken skin.
It's purposely destroyed
Dreams, papers, applications
In the kitchen bin
And bloodshot scared animal eyes.
It's imploding, pressured into ash,
While never sleeping or even stopping
Because rules are always changing.
It's 136 pieces of torn papier-mâché
soul,
Too stupid, too sad, too bad
Scattered over the floor.

EVOLUTION

It's amazing when color photos just
taken drain and redden. Haze obscures
the laughing moon,
Blocking our memories of bug lit
nights.
Shadows shift in undertones,
Subtly coloring the world in deepening
hues.
I reached after you
It was all too far gone.
Strides across the parking lot now
shortened
And dagger edged words now blunted.
I stand on the shore of what could
have been
Straining to pick the memories,
Those which tendrils of mist stole
away.
We live, we learn, we grow.
We realize we're wrong
But names appear on stone

And fresh dirt churns easy.
Time has no regard for little human
lives.

# OVERTHINKING

You breathe sideways
A movement pregnant with meaning
To the needle of my mind

# WALLFLOWER

I write my replies,
Preemptive social suicide.
Before I speak
My mind wanders.
There must be a million
Prismatic dots
Rolled onto that wall.
If I could,
I would
Disperse into them all.

# TODAY YOU WON

Today I wondered
What I'd done to survive this long.
How have I
Kept seeing blue skies?
Thoughts kept quiet,
Crept steadily forward.
You weren't there
But I felt you at my back.
Your voice becoming
The beat to my degenerative drum.
Today, you won.

SEED

I swallowed a seed
Completely on accident you see
It nestled into the folds of my being
Grew within me
Ivy limbs sprinted for the Sun
I wanted to tell you not to be afraid
But my tongue is replaced
And bark hardens my veins.

# IF THEN

I'm stuck in gray matter
Mud weighing on my boots
If memories can be trusted
Then I can believe in you

# CORRUPT

I'm useless
I'm nothing
Everything I give
I let slip through my fingers
Dangle on the wind
While I wish away
Everything I've known
To hold it again

PITY PARTY

She awoke one fine cupcake morning,
Blue skies and nary a cloud in sight.
Village windows remained shuttered,
Terrific beasts tethered to the night.
It was a fine day indeed.
She had the invitations,
Colloquial and drawn in invisible ink.
Balloons of her favorite shades,
Faded blues and washed out grays,
Floated about the room;
Specters all their own.
Nine thirty and a quarter past second
five.
She clasped her hands,
Breathing anticipation,
When only a stranger's shadow
Fell upon the door.
"Am I late?"
An echo from empty marble halls.
"I do love parties after all."
She tugged at cotton candy curls

And a dress of a blander sort.
"Of course, of course.
Just lay your grievances down here.
After all, isn't that what pity parties are
for?"

# MARIONETTES

Some of us can taste the air
Others only hear static
It's simply theory
We're connected
Where you pull, my heart jerks
Subtle palpitations against the grain
I gathered the words to tell you
But you scooped them from my tongue
I dangle above our cardboard stage

# POWDERED DREAMS

Today my heart is crying
For something once received,
Simply abandoned.
Every second,
Which passes at the tick
Of two,
The distance between us
Thickens.
Swallowing our voices,
Grinding our memories
To powdered dreams.

# SOMETIMES HE'S A MAN

There's a wolf in my closet
Sometimes he's a man
He watches me through a slit
Barely there
Yet completely obvious
I can feel his eyes
Climbing each curve
Surfing the ins and outs
Crouched low like hanging smoke
He ripples between my clothing
I can hear him breathing
Deep and low
He sinks back to the shadow
I catch him in the corner of my eye
Shifting in shards of light
Maybe I'm too high
In the dark I begin to doubt
Then his nails glide along my spine
Sweet enough to make me shiver
I worry one day he'll rip it out

SCHISM

There's a rip
In who I am
Torn
By who I dream to be

# MEMORY IS A VAPOR

Memory is a vapor
Settling on my skin
Giving rise
To what has been
It's tendrils curl
Inviting
Choking
Allowing me to feel
What only just appeared

# SUM OF OUR MOMENTS

In my bones I ache
Every inch of my being screams to stay
Rattling my steps as I back away
Because we're just people
Different
Incomplete
And the sum of our moments is lost on
me

DIG

My heart is falling out of my chest.
Literally.
I try to find my grateful bones
Buried in the yard.
Mother said not to cut off my nose
But I think I look better without it.
She never mentioned my fingers,
They crumble as I dig.

# WHEN LIGHTNING STRIKES

What an amazing coincidence.
That I'd be standing here when
lightning struck.
Sure, it stings a little at first, but the
result?
I became
A multifaceted shimmering disco ball
of flame.
I'm enchanted.
I glow.
I'm Glinda the good witch if she were
slightly damaged,
Which I think we could argue she was
…
But I can't concentrate on those things
right now.
It's getting hard to breathe.
I'm coming apart at the seams.

# IMPERFECT CLAY

We are,
They say,
Made of clay.
Astral mud
And dusty stars,
Or Heavy red
Riverbank soul.
Farmed from the heart
Of what we truly are.
Molded into
What we wish To be.

# RUNNING AWAY

Running away is kind of my thing.
My life has been spent
Escaping the comfort of what I know,
Swan diving into oblivion.

ERROR

Errors I know well
More literally
They mean wandering
Meandering
Through a life
The outcome unspecified

# JAGGED EDGES

I exist in jagged spaces, the frayed
strands of jeans ripped between my
thighs
Art doesn't cover my walls, it props up
dust in corners, bits and pieces of a life
I forgot to throw away.
I exist in the breaks between puffs on a
cigarette, never fully pulling myself up
and away.
I remain suffocated by the sheer
amount of air.
I exist for no one, not even myself, and
fail to connect the dots between here
and there.
My reflection, red lips or smoky eyes
hiding thoughts much more sinister,
feigns surprise though I don't feel
anything more than recognition.
I've become so accustomed
I can't even claim myself anymore.

# DELICATE

Delicate words rest on the tips of heavy
sighs.
Elaborate silences decorate our walls.
In place of pictures we hold frames of
dust laden time.
It's a line to cross but something bars
us back.
Like a horror house of mirrors, we're
stuck with only our reflections.
Though in crowds I've found ways to
fall out of time.
In those places, filled with dozens of
blank stammering faces, I've never felt
more alone.

# SUBMERGED

There's a tide rising within me.
A radiating wave of light reflected from
the ocean floor.
I'm submerged in relief,
Grasping for air.

# IPHONE PREFERS DUCKS

I don't mean to say it so much
But sometimes this world *d*ucking
sucks.
And when I'm frustrated
I don't really want my phone to trade
my violent words
For small feathery creatures,
Perhaps in hopes it will quell raging
digits.
Somehow it works and I laugh at the
absurdity
Of our materialism
And our in love yet in loathe
relationships
With AI and short fuses.
Then I think of you
And my words come to a jumbling
stop.
I've long preferred making myself small
In hopes that avoidance of everything
big

Will render me no more than the
innocent bystander to a life
I've never felt in control of.
Maybe I've always believed
I didn't deserve the beauty you gave
me.
It doesn't erase the emptiness,
Or the memories of the last time
I truly felt home etched in my soul.
But I can't type "fuck" because iPhone
prefers ducks.

# CAN'T THINK

I can't think in this room
With every regret I've ever had
Staring back at me

HYPNOTIZED

I've never understood
People at rock shows in towering heels
But I'm mesmerized
By their sultry disregard.
I think it's odd
When families talk over dinner
Yet I'm entranced
By their shifting notes in laughter.
Once the idea
That I should be my own person,
Capable of a life beyond one
envisioned
Of me, for me, in spite of me,
Sent chills through my skin.
Somehow, here I exist,
Hypnotized, mesmerized
And I wonder Is this what normal feels
like?

# DROWNED IN THE DESERT

Your memory is a ripple in the sand
A fading oasis beyond sweltering lines
Forever sweeping away on the wind
Taut and teasing
A barrier into foreign lands
Unforgiving in the way it leads
The way it never gives
I don't dance
But memory beckons a sway or two
If only to say I drowned in the desert
And absence of you

# MAGNETIC

Just like that,
Your soul pressed into mine.
This is where we belong.

# PASSAGE

The passage of time
Of lines in the road
Or trees on the horizon
Seconds passing
Or years gliding
Through dim tunnels
And dark underbrush
How far we travel
Without realizing
How far we've come